T0064239

RED POT CHEF: COLORING BOOK

ANDRE PONDER

authorHOUSE

AuthorHouse™
1663 Liberty Drive
Bloomington, IN 47403
www.authorhouse.com
Phone: 833-262-8899

Published by AuthorHouse 03/01/2021

ISBN: 978-1-6655-1865-9 (sc)
ISBN: 978-1-6655-1864-2 (e)

Print information available on the last page.

This book is printed on acid-free paper.

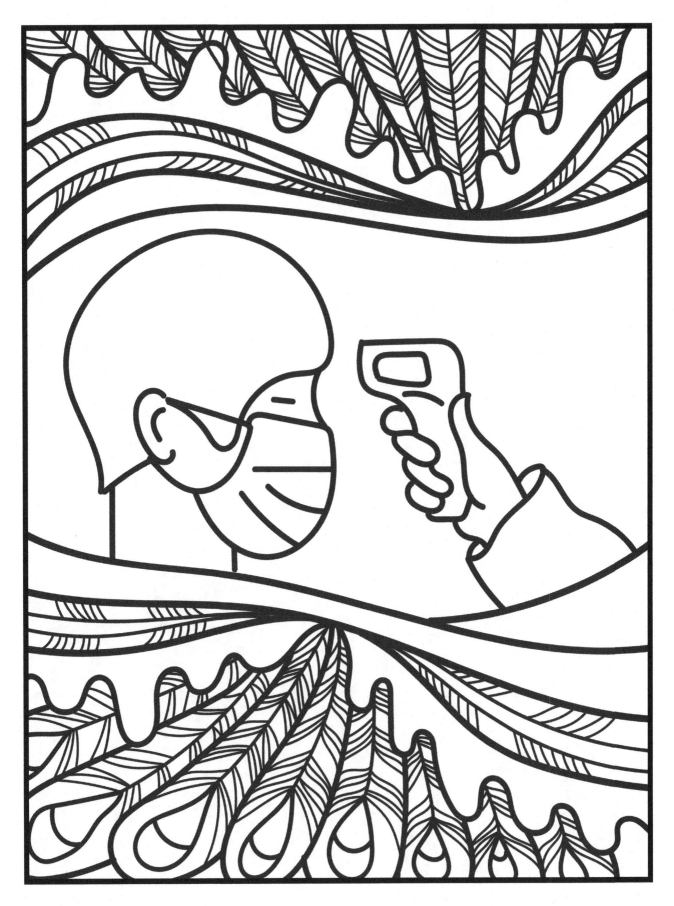

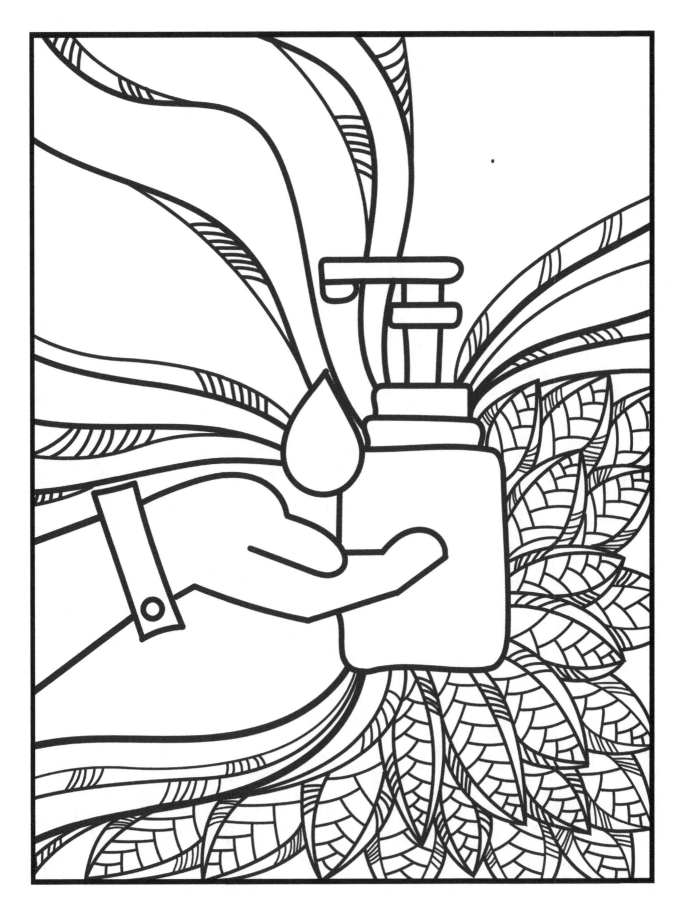

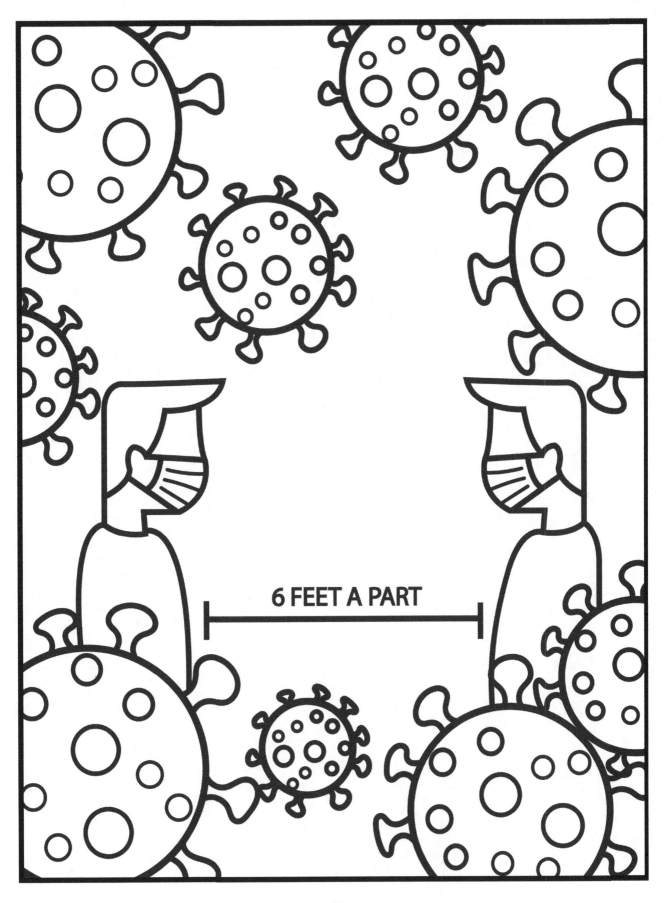

6 FEET A PART

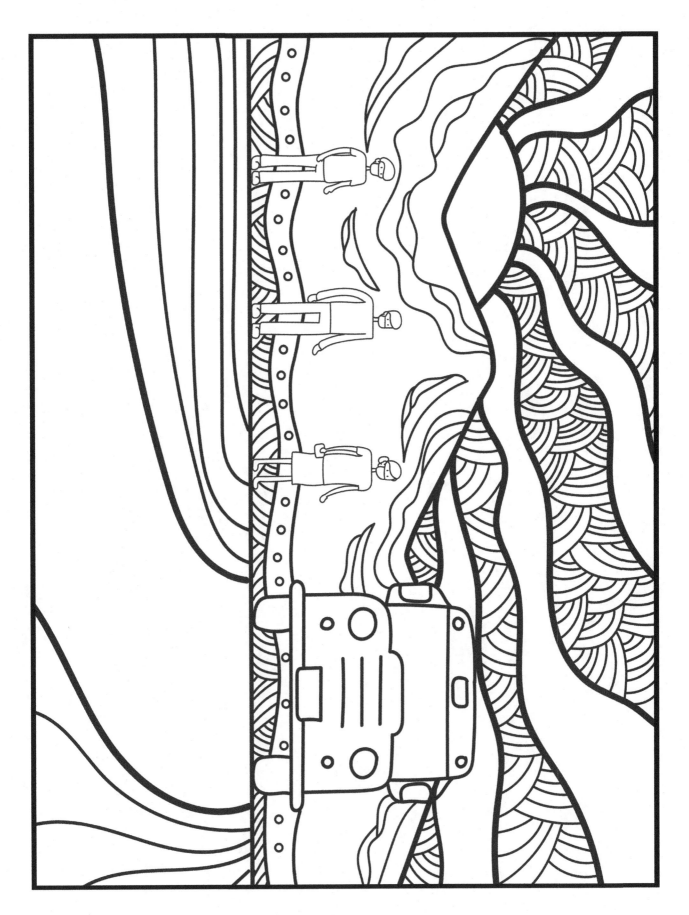

Printed in the United States
by Baker & Taylor Publisher Services